Drawing Arabians

and Other Amazing Horses

by Rae Young

CAPSTONE PRESS
a capstone imprint

Snap Books are published by Capstone Press,
1710 Roe Crest Drive, North Mankato, Minnesota 56003
www.capstonepub.com

Library of Congress Cataloging-in-Publication Data
Young, Rae.
  Drawing Arabians and other amazing horses / by Rae Young.
      pages cm. — (Snap. Drawing horses)
  Summary: "Lively text and step-by-step instructions give an introduction to drawing
horses"—Provided by publisher.
  ISBN 978-1-4765-3995-9 (library binding)
  ISBN 978-1-4765-6049-6 (eBook PDF)
1. Horses in art—Juvenile literature. 2. Arabian horse in art—Juvenile literature.
3. Drawing—Technique—Juvenile literature. I. Title.
  NC783.8.H65Y682 2014b
  743.6'96655—dc23   2013035801

Editorial Credits
Mari Bolte, editor; Lori Bye, designer; Jennifer Walker, production specialist

Photo Credits
All illustrations are by Q2AMedia Services Private Ltd, except for June Brigman, 28-29, 30-31

Printed in China by Nordica.
1013/CA21301921
092013   007745NORDS14

TABLE OF CONTENTS

GETTING STARTED

Some artists see the world as their canvas. Others see the world as their pasture! If you're a horse lover, grab a pencil and a notebook. Just pick a project and follow the step-by-step instructions. Even if you've never drawn a horse before, the projects in this book will get you started. You'll have everything you need to draw a funny foal or a record-setting racehorse.

Once you've mastered the basics, try giving your art a personal touch. Customize each horse's saddle pad or halter with bright colors and patterns. Add in details like silver conchos or textured leather. Draw accessories such as winter blankets, first-place ribbons, or buckets and brushes. Why not try drawing your friends on a trail ride or galloping across a beach? Don't be afraid to get creative!

TOOLS OF THE TRADE

1. Every artist needs something to draw on. Clean white paper is perfect for creating art. Use a drawing pad or a folder to organize your artwork.

2. Pencils are great for both simple sketches and difficult drawings. Always have one handy!

3. Finish your drawing with color! Colored pencils, markers, or even paints give your equine art detail and realism.

4. Want to add more finishing touches? Try outlining and shading your drawings with artist pens.

5. Don't be afraid of digital art! There are lots of free or inexpensive drawing apps for tablets or smartphones. Apps are a great way to experiment with different tools while on the go.

HALTER CLASS

Native horse costumes are made to set off the Arabian horse's features. Tassles, beads, and jewels make this desert horse shine in the sun.

Step 1.

Tip

Take this design to the next level by drawing the whole horse and its rider in native costume. Match the rider's outfit and head scarf with the horse's saddle, saddlecloth, and bridle.

Step 2.

Step 3.

Step 4.

CROSS COUNTRY COMPETITORS

Eventers compete in three different phases—cross country, dressage, and show jumping. The second phase, cross country, is shown here. Cross country teams must complete a course of solid jumps up and down hills, through water, and over various terrains.

Step 1.

Step 2.

Tip

The white on the horse's legs is called eventing grease. Eventing grease is applied to a horse's legs and chest before the cross country phase. This grease protects against cuts and bruises.

Step 3.

Step 4.

FOR THE CURE

Therapy horses work at rehabilitation centers, in hospitals and assisted-living facilities, and with adults and children with disabilities. Therapy horses help people heal, both mentally and physically.

Step 1.

Step 2.

Tip

Add bareback pads, special saddles, or straps called surcingles. These features can help riders feel safe on therapy horses.

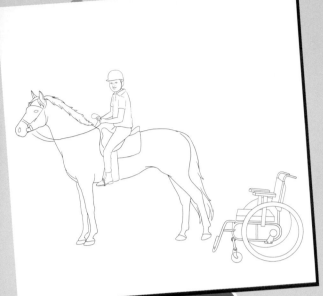

Step 3.

Step 4.

FOX HUNTER

Fox hunters follow a pack of hounds as they pursue their prey. Fox hunters must have both speed and stamina to keep up with the hunt. They also must be well trained to jump safely over fences.

Step 1.

Step 2.

Tip

Fox hunting dogs are always called hounds. English, American, Crossbred, and Penn-Marydel foxhounds are the four breeds used on the hunt. Try drawing one of each!

FACT

A fox that doesn't want to be chased hides in its den. When a fox "goes to ground," the hunt is over. Many hunts today use a fake trail, or drag, to lead the hounds.

Step 3.

Step 4.

OVERNIGHT TRIP

Do you like hunting or camping? Maybe you should get yourself a pack horse or mule! Pack animals help hunters and campers by carrying around heavy equipment. The mule's expression shows that it has traveled a long way.

Step 1.

Step 2.

Tip

Horses are easier to coax through tricky places on the trail. Mules are born followers. Most mules will follow a horse anywhere. Draw this pair in a sticky situation, such as a rocky slope or a deep gorge.

Step 3.

Step 4.

Step 5.

Step 6.

FACT

A trail horse and pack mule can travel as far as 20 miles (32 kilometers) a day.

REPORTING FOR DUTY

Police horses give officers good visibility and allow them to be on the scene quickly. They are especially useful for crowd control. Not all horses have what it takes to become a police horse. Give your police horse a brave, trustworthy look.

Step 1.

Step 2.

Tip

Help your police horse show up in a crowd with reflective gear. Add reflective reins, breastcollars, bridles, saddlebags, or leg wraps.

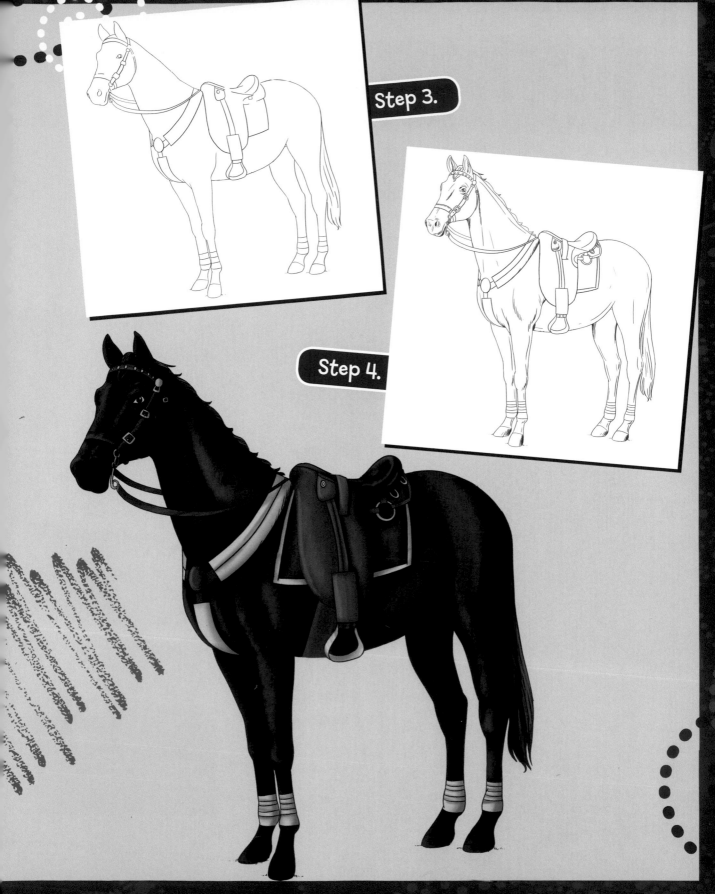

Step 3.

Step 4.

BARN PALS

Look in any barn, and you'll likely find both horses and cats. It's natural that these two animals should form a bond. Which is cuter—a happy horse or a purring cat?

Step 1.

Step 2.

Tip

Make this pair even cuter by drawing matching halters and collars.

Step 3.

Step 4.

LONG DISTANCE

The Arabian was originally bred for speed and endurance. Today it is a natural choice for an endurance horse. Draw your Arabian horse tackling tough obstacles, such as steep hills or deep rivers.

Step 1.

FACT

One of the most famous endurance races is the Tevis Cup. This 100-mile (161-km) race course takes riders through the rough Sierra Nevada Mountains in California.

Step 2.

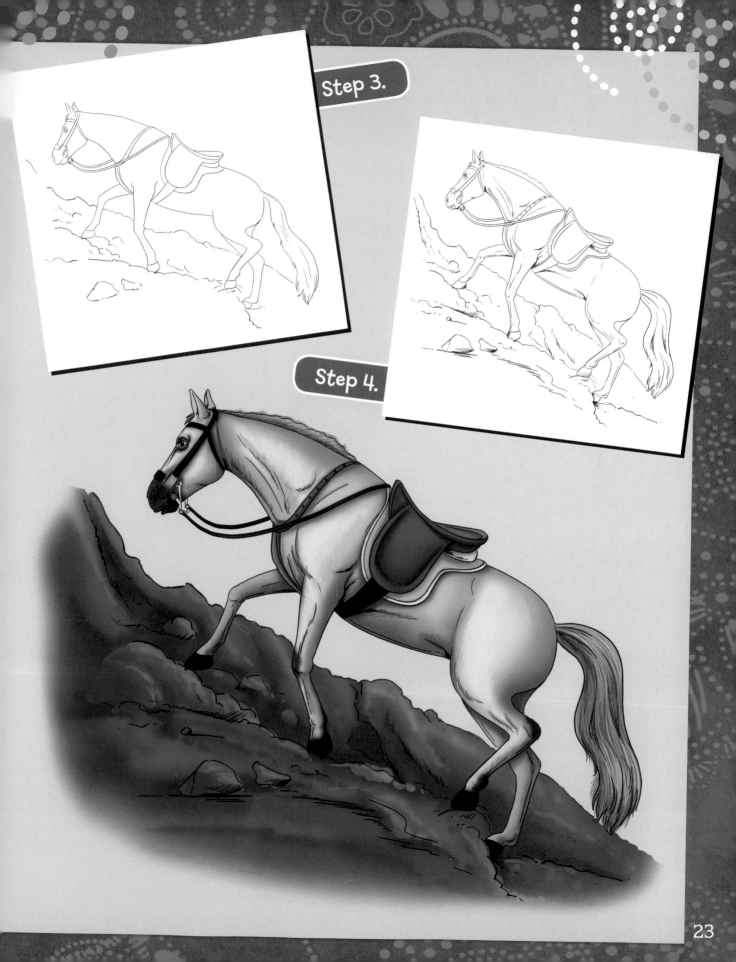

Step 3.

Step 4.

DRIVING FOR SPORT

A combined driving event (CDE) pairs the sport of three-day eventing with the fun of driving. Horses and drivers must compete in three events—dressage, marathon driving, and obstacles. Draw your combined driving pair bravely tackling a water obstacle.

Step 1.

Step 2.

Tip

Don't forget the little things! Driving whips, ear bonnets, side lamps, and safety boots are just a few items you can add for detail.

Step 3.

Step 4.

SASSY SADDLEBRED

The American saddlebred is a natural show horse. Draw this horse with a proud, high-stepping gait. The ribbons around its neck and on its bridle show that it's a winner.

Tip

Take your champion a step further by drawing the rest of its body and its long, flowing tail.

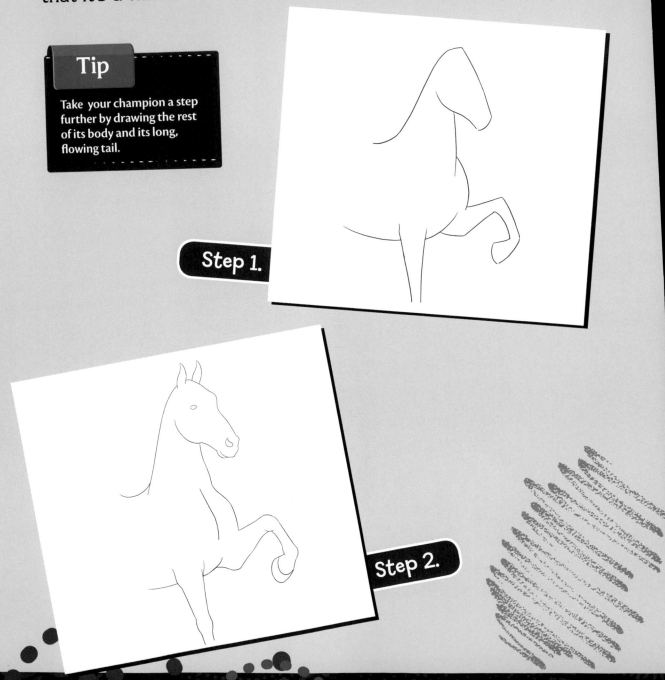

Step 1.

Step 2.

KING OF THE WIND

Arabians are the oldest horse breed. With their deep chests, straight legs, and well-developed lungs, Arabians were the perfect desert mount.

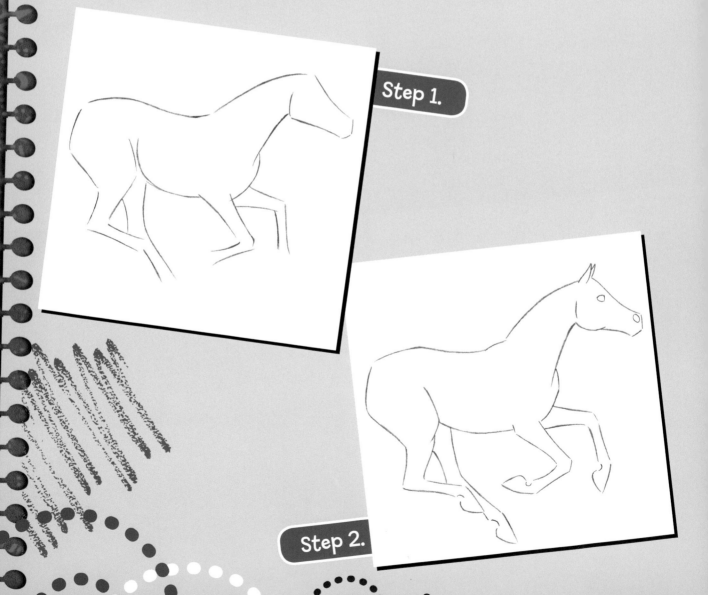

Step 1.

Step 2.

Step 4.

FACT

Arabian horses always have black skin, no matter what their coat color. This feature protects their skin in the hot desert sun.

CLIP CLOP CLYDE

Clydesdales are one of the most recognizable horse breeds. Huge bodies, enormous hooves, and fancy leg feathering help the Clydesdale stand out in a crowd.

Step 1.

Tip

Clydesdales are typically driven in pairs. So draw this one a teammate!

Step 2.

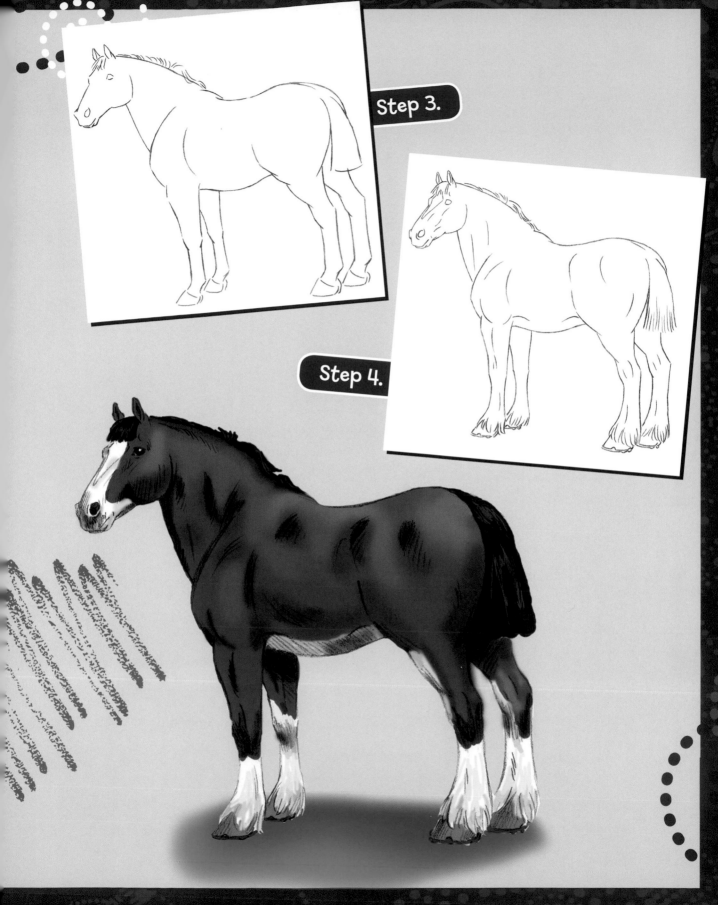

Step 3.

Step 4.

INTERNET SITES

FactHound offers a safe, fun way to find Internet sites related to this book. All of the sites on FactHound have been researched by our staff.

Here's all you do:

Visit *www.facthound.com*

Type in this code: 9781476539959

LOOK FOR ALL THE BOOKS IN THIS SERIES

Drawing Appaloosas and Other Handsome Horses

Drawing Friesians and Other Beautiful Horses

Drawing Arabians and Other Amazing Horses

Drawing Mustangs and Other Wild Horses

Drawing Barrel Racers and Other Speedy Horses

Drawing Thoroughbreds and Other Elegant Horses